If found, please return to:

How do I use TLP?

The get the most from this book, simply work through the sections, responding to the prompts provided. Do this for as many lessons as possible, and over time you will begin to develop some highly effective habits.

Planning is most powerful when done in two phases. Ideally, start your template a few days in advance, and then come back to it again the day (or morning) before the lesson. This will help you spot any parts that need reworking before you hit the classroom.

TLP is based on the principles outlined in **Lean Lesson Planning**. If you really want to become an expert planner, then I'd highly recommend getting your hands on a copy, and using it alongside this book.

I'm deeply passionate about this stuff. If you have suggestions for how this book could be improved, please do get in touch, I'd love to hear from you.

And if this book has helped you, spread the word. Tell your colleagues, write a blog-post, and if you're feeling extra-generous, leave a quick one-line review on Amazon.

Peps
pepsmccrea@gmail.com
@pepsmccrea

Class/lesson	Date/time

END POINT What do you want your students to have learnt by the end of the lesson, and how will you assess whether they've got there?

STEPS What prior knowledge are they coming in with, and what learning steps do they need to go through to successfully get to the end point?

EXPERIENCES What experiences will help your students progress through those steps, along the simplest and shortest path?

RECALL What previous learning do you want them to re-engage with, so they will remember it for longer?

EVALUTION How well did your students make progress towards their end point, and what might you do differently in future?

Teacher Lesson Planner

Class/lesson	Date/time

END POINT What do you want your students to have learnt by the end of the lesson, and how will you assess whether they've got there?

STEPS What prior knowledge are they coming in with, and what learning steps do they need to go through to successfully get to the end point?

EXPERIENCES What experiences will help your students progress through those steps, along the simplest and shortest path?

RECALL What previous learning do you want them to re-engage with, so they will remember it for longer?

EVALUTION How well did your students make progress towards their end point, and what might you do differently in future?

Class/lesson	Date/time

END POINT What do you want your students to have learnt by the end of the lesson, and how will you assess whether they've got there?

STEPS What prior knowledge are they coming in with, and what learning steps do they need to go through to successfully get to the end point?

EXPERIENCES What experiences will help your students progress through those steps, along the simplest and shortest path?

RECALL What previous learning do you want them to re-engage with, so they will remember it for longer?

EVALUTION How well did your students make progress towards their end point, and what might you do differently in future?

Class/lesson	Date/time

END POINT What do you want your students to have learnt by the end of the lesson, and how will you assess whether they've got there?

STEPS What prior knowledge are they coming in with, and what learning steps do they need to go through to successfully get to the end point?

EXPERIENCES What experiences will help your students progress through those steps, along the simplest and shortest path?

RECALL What previous learning do you want them to re-engage with, so they will remember it for longer?

EVALUTION How well did your students make progress towards their end point, and what might you do differently in future?

Class/lesson	Date/time

END POINT What do you want your students to have learnt by the end of the lesson, and how will you assess whether they've got there?

STEPS What prior knowledge are they coming in with, and what learning steps do they need to go through to successfully get to the end point?

EXPERIENCES What experiences will help your students progress through those steps, along the simplest and shortest path?

RECALL What previous learning do you want them to re-engage with, so they will remember it for longer?

EVALUTION How well did your students make progress towards their end point, and what might you do differently in future?

Class/lesson	Date/time

END POINT What do you want your students to have learnt by the end of the lesson, and how will you assess whether they've got there?

STEPS What prior knowledge are they coming in with, and what learning steps do they need to go through to successfully get to the end point?

EXPERIENCES What experiences will help your students progress through those steps, along the simplest and shortest path?

RECALL What previous learning do you want them to re-engage with, so they will remember it for longer?

EVALUTION How well did your students make progress towards their end point, and what might you do differently in future?

Class/lesson	Date/time

END POINT What do you want your students to have learnt by the end of the lesson, and how will you assess whether they've got there?

STEPS What prior knowledge are they coming in with, and what learning steps do they need to go through to successfully get to the end point?

EXPERIENCES What experiences will help your students progress through those steps, along the simplest and shortest path?

RECALL What previous learning do you want them to re-engage with, so they will remember it for longer?

EVALUTION How well did your students make progress towards their end point, and what might you do differently in future?

Teacher Lesson Planner

| Class/lesson | Date/time |

END POINT What do you want your students to have learnt by the end of the lesson, and how will you assess whether they've got there?

STEPS What prior knowledge are they coming in with, and what learning steps do they need to go through to successfully get to the end point?

EXPERIENCES What experiences will help your students progress through those steps, along the simplest and shortest path?

RECALL What previous learning do you want them to re-engage with, so they will remember it for longer?

EVALUTION How well did your students make progress towards their end point, and what might you do differently in future?

Class/lesson	Date/time

END POINT What do you want your students to have learnt by the end of the lesson, and how will you assess whether they've got there?

STEPS What prior knowledge are they coming in with, and what learning steps do they need to go through to successfully get to the end point?

EXPERIENCES What experiences will help your students progress through those steps, along the simplest and shortest path?

RECALL What previous learning do you want them to re-engage with, so they will remember it for longer?

EVALUTION How well did your students make progress towards their end point, and what might you do differently in future?

Class/lesson	Date/time

END POINT What do you want your students to have learnt by the end of the lesson, and how will you assess whether they've got there?

STEPS What prior knowledge are they coming in with, and what learning steps do they need to go through to successfully get to the end point?

EXPERIENCES What experiences will help your students progress through those steps, along the simplest and shortest path?

RECALL What previous learning do you want them to re-engage with, so they will remember it for longer?

EVALUTION How well did your students make progress towards their end point, and what might you do differently in future?

Class/lesson	Date/time

END POINT What do you want your students to have learnt by the end of the lesson, and how will you assess whether they've got there?

STEPS What prior knowledge are they coming in with, and what learning steps do they need to go through to successfully get to the end point?

EXPERIENCES What experiences will help your students progress through those steps, along the simplest and shortest path?

RECALL What previous learning do you want them to re-engage with, so they will remember it for longer?

EVALUTION How well did your students make progress towards their end point, and what might you do differently in future?

Class/lesson	Date/time

END POINT What do you want your students to have learnt by the end of the lesson, and how will you assess whether they've got there?

STEPS What prior knowledge are they coming in with, and what learning steps do they need to go through to successfully get to the end point?

EXPERIENCES What experiences will help your students progress through those steps, along the simplest and shortest path?

RECALL What previous learning do you want them to re-engage with, so they will remember it for longer?

EVALUTION How well did your students make progress towards their end point, and what might you do differently in future?

Class/lesson	Date/time

END POINT What do you want your students to have learnt by the end of the lesson, and how will you assess whether they've got there?

STEPS What prior knowledge are they coming in with, and what learning steps do they need to go through to successfully get to the end point?

EXPERIENCES What experiences will help your students progress through those steps, along the simplest and shortest path?

RECALL What previous learning do you want them to re-engage with, so they will remember it for longer?

EVALUTION How well did your students make progress towards their end point, and what might you do differently in future?

Class/lesson	Date/time

END POINT What do you want your students to have learnt by the end of the lesson, and how will you assess whether they've got there?

STEPS What prior knowledge are they coming in with, and what learning steps do they need to go through to successfully get to the end point?

EXPERIENCES What experiences will help your students progress through those steps, along the simplest and shortest path?

RECALL What previous learning do you want them to re-engage with, so they will remember it for longer?

EVALUTION How well did your students make progress towards their end point, and what might you do differently in future?

Teacher Lesson Planner

Class/lesson	Date/time

END POINT What do you want your students to have learnt by the end of the lesson, and how will you assess whether they've got there?

STEPS What prior knowledge are they coming in with, and what learning steps do they need to go through to successfully get to the end point?

EXPERIENCES What experiences will help your students progress through those steps, along the simplest and shortest path?

RECALL What previous learning do you want them to re-engage with, so they will remember it for longer?

EVALUTION How well did your students make progress towards their end point, and what might you do differently in future?

Class/lesson	Date/time

END POINT What do you want your students to have learnt by the end of the lesson, and how will you assess whether they've got there?

STEPS What prior knowledge are they coming in with, and what learning steps do they need to go through to successfully get to the end point?

EXPERIENCES What experiences will help your students progress through those steps, along the simplest and shortest path?

RECALL What previous learning do you want them to re-engage with, so they will remember it for longer?

EVALUTION How well did your students make progress towards their end point, and what might you do differently in future?

Class/lesson	Date/time

END POINT What do you want your students to have learnt by the end of the lesson, and how will you assess whether they've got there?

STEPS What prior knowledge are they coming in with, and what learning steps do they need to go through to successfully get to the end point?

EXPERIENCES What experiences will help your students progress through those steps, along the simplest and shortest path?

RECALL What previous learning do you want them to re-engage with, so they will remember it for longer?

EVALUTION How well did your students make progress towards their end point, and what might you do differently in future?

Class/lesson	Date/time

END POINT What do you want your students to have learnt by the end of the lesson, and how will you assess whether they've got there?

STEPS What prior knowledge are they coming in with, and what learning steps do they need to go through to successfully get to the end point?

EXPERIENCES What experiences will help your students progress through those steps, along the simplest and shortest path?

RECALL What previous learning do you want them to re-engage with, so they will remember it for longer?

EVALUTION How well did your students make progress towards their end point, and what might you do differently in future?

Class/lesson	Date/time

END POINT What do you want your students to have learnt by the end of the lesson, and how will you assess whether they've got there?

STEPS What prior knowledge are they coming in with, and what learning steps do they need to go through to successfully get to the end point?

EXPERIENCES What experiences will help your students progress through those steps, along the simplest and shortest path?

RECALL What previous learning do you want them to re-engage with, so they will remember it for longer?

EVALUTION How well did your students make progress towards their end point, and what might you do differently in future?

Class/lesson	Date/time

END POINT What do you want your students to have learnt by the end of the lesson, and how will you assess whether they've got there?

STEPS What prior knowledge are they coming in with, and what learning steps do they need to go through to successfully get to the end point?

EXPERIENCES What experiences will help your students progress through those steps, along the simplest and shortest path?

RECALL What previous learning do you want them to re-engage with, so they will remember it for longer?

EVALUTION How well did your students make progress towards their end point, and what might you do differently in future?

Class/lesson	Date/time

END POINT What do you want your students to have learnt by the end of the lesson, and how will you assess whether they've got there?

STEPS What prior knowledge are they coming in with, and what learning steps do they need to go through to successfully get to the end point?

EXPERIENCES What experiences will help your students progress through those steps, along the simplest and shortest path?

RECALL What previous learning do you want them to re-engage with, so they will remember it for longer?

EVALUTION How well did your students make progress towards their end point, and what might you do differently in future?

Class/lesson	Date/time

END POINT What do you want your students to have learnt by the end of the lesson, and how will you assess whether they've got there?

STEPS What prior knowledge are they coming in with, and what learning steps do they need to go through to successfully get to the end point?

EXPERIENCES What experiences will help your students progress through those steps, along the simplest and shortest path?

RECALL What previous learning do you want them to re-engage with, so they will remember it for longer?

EVALUTION How well did your students make progress towards their end point, and what might you do differently in future?

Class/lesson	Date/time

END POINT What do you want your students to have learnt by the end of the lesson, and how will you assess whether they've got there?

STEPS What prior knowledge are they coming in with, and what learning steps do they need to go through to successfully get to the end point?

EXPERIENCES What experiences will help your students progress through those steps, along the simplest and shortest path?

RECALL What previous learning do you want them to re-engage with, so they will remember it for longer?

EVALUTION How well did your students make progress towards their end point, and what might you do differently in future?

Teacher Lesson Planner

Class/lesson	Date/time

END POINT What do you want your students to have learnt by the end of the lesson, and how will you assess whether they've got there?

STEPS What prior knowledge are they coming in with, and what learning steps do they need to go through to successfully get to the end point?

EXPERIENCES What experiences will help your students progress through those steps, along the simplest and shortest path?

RECALL What previous learning do you want them to re-engage with, so they will remember it for longer?

EVALUTION How well did your students make progress towards their end point, and what might you do differently in future?

Class/lesson	Date/time

END POINT What do you want your students to have learnt by the end of the lesson, and how will you assess whether they've got there?

STEPS What prior knowledge are they coming in with, and what learning steps do they need to go through to successfully get to the end point?

EXPERIENCES What experiences will help your students progress through those steps, along the simplest and shortest path?

RECALL What previous learning do you want them to re-engage with, so they will remember it for longer?

EVALUTION How well did your students make progress towards their end point, and what might you do differently in future?

Teacher Lesson Planner

Class/lesson	Date/time

END POINT What do you want your students to have learnt by the end of the lesson, and how will you assess whether they've got there?

STEPS What prior knowledge are they coming in with, and what learning steps do they need to go through to successfully get to the end point?

EXPERIENCES What experiences will help your students progress through those steps, along the simplest and shortest path?

RECALL What previous learning do you want them to re-engage with, so they will remember it for longer?

EVALUTION How well did your students make progress towards their end point, and what might you do differently in future?

Class/lesson	Date/time

END POINT What do you want your students to have learnt by the end of the lesson, and how will you assess whether they've got there?

STEPS What prior knowledge are they coming in with, and what learning steps do they need to go through to successfully get to the end point?

EXPERIENCES What experiences will help your students progress through those steps, along the simplest and shortest path?

RECALL What previous learning do you want them to re-engage with, so they will remember it for longer?

EVALUTION How well did your students make progress towards their end point, and what might you do differently in future?

Class/lesson	Date/time

END POINT What do you want your students to have learnt by the end of the lesson, and how will you assess whether they've got there?

STEPS What prior knowledge are they coming in with, and what learning steps do they need to go through to successfully get to the end point?

EXPERIENCES What experiences will help your students progress through those steps, along the simplest and shortest path?

RECALL What previous learning do you want them to re-engage with, so they will remember it for longer?

EVALUTION How well did your students make progress towards their end point, and what might you do differently in future?

Class/lesson	Date/time

END POINT What do you want your students to have learnt by the end of the lesson, and how will you assess whether they've got there?

STEPS What prior knowledge are they coming in with, and what learning steps do they need to go through to successfully get to the end point?

EXPERIENCES What experiences will help your students progress through those steps, along the simplest and shortest path?

RECALL What previous learning do you want them to re-engage with, so they will remember it for longer?

EVALUTION How well did your students make progress towards their end point, and what might you do differently in future?

Class/lesson	Date/time

END POINT What do you want your students to have learnt by the end of the lesson, and how will you assess whether they've got there?

STEPS What prior knowledge are they coming in with, and what learning steps do they need to go through to successfully get to the end point?

EXPERIENCES What experiences will help your students progress through those steps, along the simplest and shortest path?

RECALL What previous learning do you want them to re-engage with, so they will remember it for longer?

EVALUTION How well did your students make progress towards their end point, and what might you do differently in future?

Teacher Lesson Planner

Class/lesson	Date/time

END POINT What do you want your students to have learnt by the end of the lesson, and how will you assess whether they've got there?

STEPS What prior knowledge are they coming in with, and what learning steps do they need to go through to successfully get to the end point?

EXPERIENCES What experiences will help your students progress through those steps, along the simplest and shortest path?

RECALL What previous learning do you want them to re-engage with, so they will remember it for longer?

EVALUTION How well did your students make progress towards their end point, and what might you do differently in future?

Class/lesson	Date/time

END POINT What do you want your students to have learnt by the end of the lesson, and how will you assess whether they've got there?

STEPS What prior knowledge are they coming in with, and what learning steps do they need to go through to successfully get to the end point?

EXPERIENCES What experiences will help your students progress through those steps, along the simplest and shortest path?

RECALL What previous learning do you want them to re-engage with, so they will remember it for longer?

EVALUTION How well did your students make progress towards their end point, and what might you do differently in future?

Class/lesson	Date/time

END POINT What do you want your students to have learnt by the end of the lesson, and how will you assess whether they've got there?

STEPS What prior knowledge are they coming in with, and what learning steps do they need to go through to successfully get to the end point?

EXPERIENCES What experiences will help your students progress through those steps, along the simplest and shortest path?

RECALL What previous learning do you want them to re-engage with, so they will remember it for longer?

EVALUTION How well did your students make progress towards their end point, and what might you do differently in future?

Class/lesson	Date/time

END POINT What do you want your students to have learnt by the end of the lesson, and how will you assess whether they've got there?

STEPS What prior knowledge are they coming in with, and what learning steps do they need to go through to successfully get to the end point?

EXPERIENCES What experiences will help your students progress through those steps, along the simplest and shortest path?

RECALL What previous learning do you want them to re-engage with, so they will remember it for longer?

EVALUTION How well did your students make progress towards their end point, and what might you do differently in future?

Class/lesson	Date/time

END POINT What do you want your students to have learnt by the end of the lesson, and how will you assess whether they've got there?

STEPS What prior knowledge are they coming in with, and what learning steps do they need to go through to successfully get to the end point?

EXPERIENCES What experiences will help your students progress through those steps, along the simplest and shortest path?

RECALL What previous learning do you want them to re-engage with, so they will remember it for longer?

EVALUTION How well did your students make progress towards their end point, and what might you do differently in future?

Class/lesson	Date/time

END POINT What do you want your students to have learnt by the end of the lesson, and how will you assess whether they've got there?

STEPS What prior knowledge are they coming in with, and what learning steps do they need to go through to successfully get to the end point?

EXPERIENCES What experiences will help your students progress through those steps, along the simplest and shortest path?

RECALL What previous learning do you want them to re-engage with, so they will remember it for longer?

EVALUTION How well did your students make progress towards their end point, and what might you do differently in future?

Class/lesson	Date/time

END POINT What do you want your students to have learnt by the end of the lesson, and how will you assess whether they've got there?

STEPS What prior knowledge are they coming in with, and what learning steps do they need to go through to successfully get to the end point?

EXPERIENCES What experiences will help your students progress through those steps, along the simplest and shortest path?

RECALL What previous learning do you want them to re-engage with, so they will remember it for longer?

EVALUTION How well did your students make progress towards their end point, and what might you do differently in future?

Class/lesson	Date/time

END POINT What do you want your students to have learnt by the end of the lesson, and how will you assess whether they've got there?

STEPS What prior knowledge are they coming in with, and what learning steps do they need to go through to successfully get to the end point?

EXPERIENCES What experiences will help your students progress through those steps, along the simplest and shortest path?

RECALL What previous learning do you want them to re-engage with, so they will remember it for longer?

EVALUTION How well did your students make progress towards their end point, and what might you do differently in future?

Class/lesson	Date/time

END POINT What do you want your students to have learnt by the end of the lesson, and how will you assess whether they've got there?

STEPS What prior knowledge are they coming in with, and what learning steps do they need to go through to successfully get to the end point?

EXPERIENCES What experiences will help your students progress through those steps, along the simplest and shortest path?

RECALL What previous learning do you want them to re-engage with, so they will remember it for longer?

EVALUTION How well did your students make progress towards their end point, and what might you do differently in future?

Class/lesson	Date/time

END POINT What do you want your students to have learnt by the end of the lesson, and how will you assess whether they've got there?

STEPS What prior knowledge are they coming in with, and what learning steps do they need to go through to successfully get to the end point?

EXPERIENCES What experiences will help your students progress through those steps, along the simplest and shortest path?

RECALL What previous learning do you want them to re-engage with, so they will remember it for longer?

EVALUTION How well did your students make progress towards their end point, and what might you do differently in future?

Class/lesson	Date/time

END POINT What do you want your students to have learnt by the end of the lesson, and how will you assess whether they've got there?

STEPS What prior knowledge are they coming in with, and what learning steps do they need to go through to successfully get to the end point?

EXPERIENCES What experiences will help your students progress through those steps, along the simplest and shortest path?

RECALL What previous learning do you want them to re-engage with, so they will remember it for longer?

EVALUTION How well did your students make progress towards their end point, and what might you do differently in future?

Class/lesson	Date/time

END POINT What do you want your students to have learnt by the end of the lesson, and how will you assess whether they've got there?

STEPS What prior knowledge are they coming in with, and what learning steps do they need to go through to successfully get to the end point?

EXPERIENCES What experiences will help your students progress through those steps, along the simplest and shortest path?

RECALL What previous learning do you want them to re-engage with, so they will remember it for longer?

EVALUTION How well did your students make progress towards their end point, and what might you do differently in future?

Class/lesson	Date/time

END POINT What do you want your students to have learnt by the end of the lesson, and how will you assess whether they've got there?

STEPS What prior knowledge are they coming in with, and what learning steps do they need to go through to successfully get to the end point?

EXPERIENCES What experiences will help your students progress through those steps, along the simplest and shortest path?

RECALL What previous learning do you want them to re-engage with, so they will remember it for longer?

EVALUTION How well did your students make progress towards their end point, and what might you do differently in future?

Class/lesson	Date/time

END POINT What do you want your students to have learnt by the end of the lesson, and how will you assess whether they've got there?

STEPS What prior knowledge are they coming in with, and what learning steps do they need to go through to successfully get to the end point?

EXPERIENCES What experiences will help your students progress through those steps, along the simplest and shortest path?

RECALL What previous learning do you want them to re-engage with, so they will remember it for longer?

EVALUTION How well did your students make progress towards their end point, and what might you do differently in future?

Teacher Lesson Planner

Class/lesson	Date/time

END POINT What do you want your students to have learnt by the end of the lesson, and how will you assess whether they've got there?

STEPS What prior knowledge are they coming in with, and what learning steps do they need to go through to successfully get to the end point?

EXPERIENCES What experiences will help your students progress through those steps, along the simplest and shortest path?

RECALL What previous learning do you want them to re-engage with, so they will remember it for longer?

EVALUTION How well did your students make progress towards their end point, and what might you do differently in future?

Class/lesson	Date/time

END POINT What do you want your students to have learnt by the end of the lesson, and how will you assess whether they've got there?

STEPS What prior knowledge are they coming in with, and what learning steps do they need to go through to successfully get to the end point?

EXPERIENCES What experiences will help your students progress through those steps, along the simplest and shortest path?

RECALL What previous learning do you want them to re-engage with, so they will remember it for longer?

EVALUTION How well did your students make progress towards their end point, and what might you do differently in future?

Class/lesson	Date/time

END POINT What do you want your students to have learnt by the end of the lesson, and how will you assess whether they've got there?

STEPS What prior knowledge are they coming in with, and what learning steps do they need to go through to successfully get to the end point?

EXPERIENCES What experiences will help your students progress through those steps, along the simplest and shortest path?

RECALL What previous learning do you want them to re-engage with, so they will remember it for longer?

EVALUTION How well did your students make progress towards their end point, and what might you do differently in future?

Class/lesson	Date/time

END POINT What do you want your students to have learnt by the end of the lesson, and how will you assess whether they've got there?

STEPS What prior knowledge are they coming in with, and what learning steps do they need to go through to successfully get to the end point?

EXPERIENCES What experiences will help your students progress through those steps, along the simplest and shortest path?

RECALL What previous learning do you want them to re-engage with, so they will remember it for longer?

EVALUTION How well did your students make progress towards their end point, and what might you do differently in future?

Teacher Lesson Planner

Class/lesson	Date/time

END POINT What do you want your students to have learnt by the end of the lesson, and how will you assess whether they've got there?

STEPS What prior knowledge are they coming in with, and what learning steps do they need to go through to successfully get to the end point?

EXPERIENCES What experiences will help your students progress through those steps, along the simplest and shortest path?

RECALL What previous learning do you want them to re-engage with, so they will remember it for longer?

EVALUTION How well did your students make progress towards their end point, and what might you do differently in future?

Class/lesson	Date/time

END POINT What do you want your students to have learnt by the end of the lesson, and how will you assess whether they've got there?

STEPS What prior knowledge are they coming in with, and what learning steps do they need to go through to successfully get to the end point?

EXPERIENCES What experiences will help your students progress through those steps, along the simplest and shortest path?

RECALL What previous learning do you want them to re-engage with, so they will remember it for longer?

EVALUTION How well did your students make progress towards their end point, and what might you do differently in future?

About Peps

Peps Mccrea is an award-winning teacher educator, author and social entrepreneur.

He is a Senior Lecturer in Teacher Education at a large University in the UK, and co-founder of edtech startups Staffrm and Numeracy Ready.

Peps has three Masters degrees, two small kids, and dances like no one is watching, which is probably for the best.

Visit pepsmccrea.com for the full shebang.

Lesson Observation **Feedback Book**

An essential resource for any teacher interested in getting better

Peps Mccrea

Lean Lesson Planning

A practical approach to doing less and achieving more in the classroom

Peps Mccrea

Notes to self

Printed in Great Britain
by Amazon